The Moon

by Tess Mason

PEARSON

Scott
Foresman

Editorial Offices: Glenview, Illinois • Parsippany, New Jersey • New York, New York
Sales Offices: Needham, Massachusetts • Duluth, Georgia • Glenview, Illinois
Coppell, Texas • Ontario, California • Mesa, Arizona

ISBN: 0-328-13499-6

6 7 8 9 10 V0G1 14 13 12 11 10 09 08 07

☾ Earth's Neighbor

Humans have always been interested in the moon. The moon is our closest neighbor. Look up from the **horizon** into the night sky. The moon appears as the largest object in the sky.

Some people have worshipped the moon. The Romans may have worshipped Diana as the goddess of the moon. The Greeks called their moon goddess Artemis. Some people thought they could see a face on the moon's surface. This feature has been called "the Man in the Moon." People finally made rocket ships to fly to the moon. Getting to know our closest neighbor is an ongoing and exciting journey.

Artemis (left) was the Greek goddess of the moon. A wolf howls at the moon (below).

Moon versus Earth

The moon is Earth's only natural satellite. A satellite is an object that orbits, or moves around, another object. The moon orbits Earth, as Earth orbits the sun. We say that the moon is a *natural* satellite because it is not man-made.

The moon orbits around Earth.

The moon appears to be quite large due to its closeness to Earth. It is actually much smaller than Earth. Think of a basketball and a tennis ball. The basketball represents Earth. The tennis ball represents the moon.

The moon differs from Earth in other ways as well. Much of Earth is covered in water. But the moon has no water. The moon also has no atmosphere. On the moon, because there is no air, there is no weather.

Astronomers, or people who study outer space, first thought the dark areas that they saw on the moon might be seas. These areas are actually lava flows that cooled and hardened. Today astronomers still call them seas, such as the Sea of Tranquility. The moon's surface, or the **lunar** surface, is covered with craters, or holes. Some are more than one hundred miles across.

There are craters on the moon.

☾ Phases of the Moon

We only see the moon when the sun shines on it. And we only see one side of the moon. Different parts of the moon receive sunlight as it orbits Earth. This causes the phases of the moon.

Sometimes, the moon is almost in a line between Earth and the sun. This stops sunlight from reaching the side of the moon facing us. It makes the moon seem to vanish. This phase is called the New Moon.

As days go by, more of the sunlit moon can be seen. The moon is said to be waxing. The waxing Crescent Moon comes after the New Moon. Then, a few days later, the First Quarter Moon appears. The next phase is the waxing Gibbous Moon. Now more than half of the moon appears, but not quite a whole circle.

Finally, the entire side of the moon facing us is lit. The moon appears as a full circle, or as the Full Moon. Then the moon stops waxing and begins waning. Waning is when the moon appears to get smaller. The moon goes back through its phases during waning.

The moon's phases as they appear from Earth

Full Moon

Gibbous Moon (waning)   Gibbous Moon (waxing)

Last Quarter (waning)   First Quarter (waxing)

Crescent Moon (waning)   Crescent Moon (waxing)

New Moon

7

☾ Eclipses

The moon plays an important part in eclipses. An eclipse occurs when an object in space moves in front of another object in space. As you know, the moon orbits Earth, as Earth orbits the sun. When Earth passes between the moon and the sun, it makes a shadow on the moon. This is called a lunar eclipse. The moon can still be seen in a lunar eclipse. It turns a reddish, copper color because of Earth's shadow.

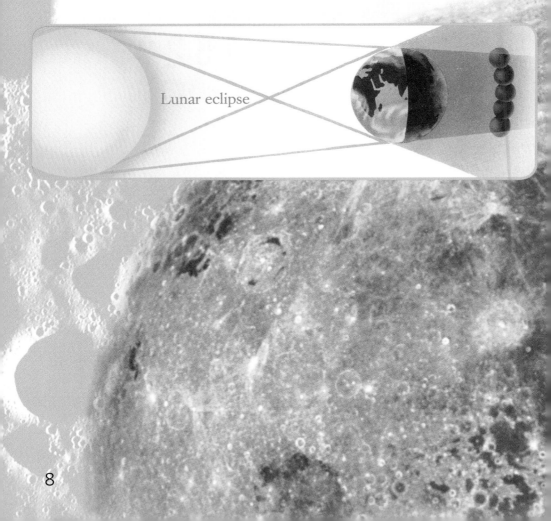

Lunar eclipse

When the moon passes between Earth and the sun, the moon blocks out the sunlight for a few minutes. This is called a solar eclipse. If the moon blocks out just a part of the sun, it is called a partial eclipse. If it covers the entire sun, it is called a total eclipse. During a total solar eclipse, you can see the sun's corona, or outer layer. You normally can't see the corona because the sun is too bright to look at without the moon blocking its rays.

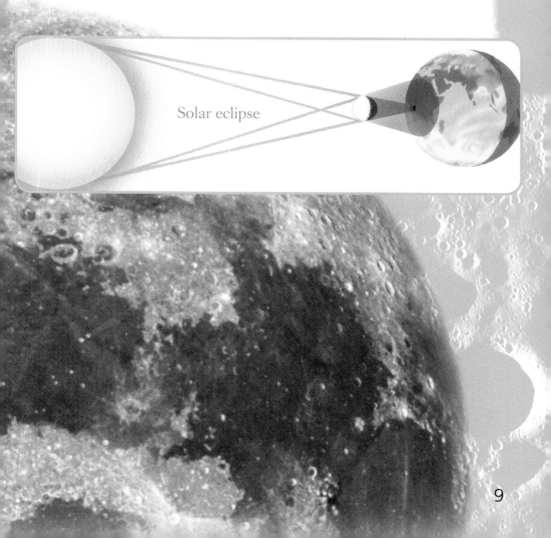

Solar eclipse

☾ Journey to the Moon

For many years scientists have used telescopes to learn about the moon. But they could not find out everything they needed to know this way. People wanted to go to the moon.

By the late 1940s, the United States and the Soviet Union were involved in the Cold War. The Cold War did not lead to actual fighting. It was a fight over political systems and ideas.

On October 4, 1957, the Soviet Union launched Sputnik 1, the world's first man-made satellite. The United States felt the need to compete. The launch of Sputnik 1 began the space race.

A scientist works on Sputnik 1.

In order to travel from Earth to the moon, scientists needed something to propel, or push, a ship there and back again. Making a powerful rocket was the best solution.

Rockets have a long history. Thousands of years ago, the Chinese invented gunpowder, which came before rockets. The first actual rocket was a Chinese fire arrow, invented before 1232. People made rockets for hundreds of years before they understood the science behind them.

Fire rocket

Chinese firecracker

A rocket is a chamber that holds a gas under pressure. A small opening at one end of the chamber allows the gas to escape. This propels, or moves, the rocket in the opposite direction of the escaping gas.

Think of a balloon. The gas in it is air. The chamber is the wall of the balloon. The rubber walls of the balloon put pressure on the air. If you poke a hole in the balloon, the pressure causes the air to escape. The balloon flies off. Rockets are an advanced version of this idea.

In the 1900s, scientists used liquid fuel to propel the rockets. The Saturn V rocket was the largest rocket ever built by the United States.

The Saturn V rocket was made to send a crew to the moon.

The John F. Kennedy Space Center
at Cape Canaveral, Florida

On October 1, 1958, the National Aeronautics
and Space Administration, or NASA, was formed. On
May 25, 1961, President John F. Kennedy announced
that the United States would commit itself to landing
an **astronaut** on the moon before the end of the
decade.

The Soviets still led the space race, though. They
put the first person into space. On April 12, 1961,
Soviet Yury Gagarin completed one orbit of Earth in
the Vostok 1. It was a small vehicle, or **capsule.** On
February 20, 1962, John H. Glenn, Jr. became the first
U.S. astronaut to orbit Earth.

In the 1960s, the NASA space flight project known as Gemini used two astronauts to practice flight in space. The astronauts tested such operations as docking with spacecraft and moving both inside and outside of the spacecraft. On June 3, 1965, Edward H. White II became the first U.S. astronaut to conduct a space walk. He was connected to the spacecraft by a tether, or cord.

NASA kept working toward its goal of landing a man on the moon before the end of the 1960s. NASA's Apollo program was designed to land men on the moon and then bring them safely back to Earth.

Apollo missions 1 to 10 provided the final links for the trip to the moon. They tested the Saturn V rocket systems that would propel the spaceship to the moon. Sadly, not all the test missions went smoothly. A fire on board Apollo 1 caused three astronauts to lose their lives. NASA quickly corrected the problems that led to the fire, so that later astronauts were safe. On Apollo 8, the first humans orbited the moon. Now, the next big step was to land.

Astronauts get ready for space travel.

Edward H. White II was connected
to the spacecraft by a tether in
the first American space walk.

☾ Apollo 11 and the Moon Today

NASA was ready to land on the moon with the Apollo 11 mission. The crew consisted of commander Neil A. Armstrong, lunar **module** pilot Edwin E. "Buzz" Aldrin, Jr., and command module pilot Michael Collins. The command module *Columbia* was the crew's main living quarters. Its service module contained supplies. The lunar module *Eagle* was the landing craft. The *Eagle* would be used to go down to the moon's surface and then back to the *Columbia*. On July 16, 1969, the spacecraft lifted off from Earth.

It took four days to reach the moon. When the astronauts got to the moon, Collins piloted the *Columbia*. Armstrong and Aldrin used the *Eagle* to go down to the surface of the moon. On July 20, 1969, the astronauts touched down on the surface of the moon. "The *Eagle* has landed," Armstrong said, just after he landed in the Sea of Tranquility. Then he stepped out onto the moon's surface, becoming the first human to set foot on the moon.

The Apollo 11 mission carried astronauts Neil Armstrong, Michael Collins, and Edwin "Buzz" Aldrin (left to right).

Armstrong and Aldrin collected soil and rock samples, took photographs, and did experiments. Then they used the *Eagle* to go up from the moon's surface and dock with the orbiting *Columbia* to return to Earth. After Armstrong and Aldrin joined Collins, the *Eagle* drifted off into space. It orbits the moon to this day.

Astronaut "Buzz" Aldrin takes his first walk on the Moon next to the lunar module *Eagle*.

The command module of the *Columbia* separated from its service module before entering Earth's atmosphere. On July 24, 1969, the command module splashed into the Pacific Ocean. The astronauts opened the **hatch** and exited their craft. They wore special suits and went into **quarantine,** a place or time in which people are held until it is determined that they have no diseases. After that, the astronauts were able to see their family and friends.

The service module held supplies.

The command module was the main living quarters.

The command module splashed down in the Pacific Ocean.

Six Apollo missions landed on the moon and returned to Earth. No astronauts have visited the moon since 1972.

Humans are still fascinated by the moon. NASA's space program has continued to grow since the Apollo missions. In 2004, President Bush announced a plan to return to the moon. Perhaps one day people will live and work on the moon. The moon will inspire people for centuries to come.

A space shuttle flight lifts off from Cape Canaveral, Florida.

Glossary

astronaut *n.* a member of the crew of a spacecraft.

capsule *n.* the enclosed front section of a rocket that carries astronauts, instruments, and other equipment into space.

hatch *n.* a small door or opening, as in a spaceship; the covering for such an opening.

horizon *n.* the line where Earth and sky appear to meet; skyline.

lunar *adj.* of, like, or about the moon.

module *n.* a self-contained unit or system within a larger system, often designed for a particular function.

quarantine *n.* detention, isolation, and other measures taken to prevent the spread of an infectious disease.